GETTING
The Dead
OUT

The Way to Spiritual Freedom Through the Process

of Pruning and How to Keep It!

GETTING
The Dead
OUT

The Way to Spiritual Freedom Through the Process

of Pruning and How to Keep It!

ANTHONY WALKER

CITIOFBOOKS, INC.
3736 Eubank NE Suite A1
Albuquerque, NM 87111-3579
www.citiofbooks.com
Hotline: 1 (877) 389-2759
Fax: 1 (505) 930-7244

Ordering Information:
Quantity sales. Special discounts are available on quantity purchases by corporations, associations, and others. For details, contact the publisher at the address above.

Printed in the United States of America.

ISBN-13:   Softcover   979-8-89391-172-5
                 eBook   979-8-89391-173-2

Library of Congress Control Number: 2024912706

ACKNOWLEDGMENT

Dear Editor Terry McNew, Senior Author Advisor Dee Nelson, Senior Book Fulfillment Team led by Kelsey Marquez, and all my family and friends who gave me encouragement,

I would like to express my deepest gratitude for your dedication, expertise, and hard work in bringing this book to life. Your collective efforts have truly made a difference in shaping this publication and ensuring its success.

Thank you for your invaluable contributions and unwavering support throughout this journey. I am excited to continue our collaboration and create more impactful literary works together.

Warm regards, Author Anthony Walker

TABLE OF CONTENTS

MY VISION STATEMENT

Habakkuk 2:2| KJV

"**A**nd the Lord answered me, and said, Write the vision, and make it plain upon tables, so he may run that readeth it."

My vision is to help people go Monday through Saturday without getting their brains beaten in by the world until they get back to the place they are getting fed on Sunday; and to see people get their minds, their wills, their spirits, emotions, and - the big one, - their bodies healed. We are living in the land of the dead and it does not have to be that way.

JESUS said in 2 Chronicles 7:14, "If my people, which are called by name, shall humble themselves, and pray, and seek my face, and turn from their wicked ways; then will I hear from heaven, and will forgive their sin, and will heal their land."

I want to point people back to JESUS so they can get healed and set free through GOD'S word, like I did.

INTRODUCTION

My name is Anthony Walker. I have been trimming and or pruning landscape for eight years and what I have discovered is that JESUS did not trim or prune landscape, meaning trees or bushes, but he compared people to landscape. In Matthew 12:33 JESUS compares people to trees. I wrote this book to help people understand and help them through GOD's word. Then they can get free and stay free by pruning the things in their lives that don't bring forth good fruit out of the life that **GOD** has entrusted to them.

What are the fruits? Galatians 5:22-23 tells us "The fruit of the spirit is love, joy, peace, forbearance, kindness, goodness, faithfulness, gentleness, and self-control. Against such things there is no law."

Well I guess this was a big deal to **GOD** because he uses trees in 296 verses in the Bible. GOD started out in Genesis 1:11 talking about trees. In verse 12 he talks about how good the fruit was. And then in verse 29 he tells how it will bring meat to us. In Genesis 2:16, he tells us we can eat from and of all the trees but one. He tells us in Genesis 2:17 about the one we cannot eat from or we will die. I have asked myself before which trees have I been eating from. My life reflected what tree I was eating from because I was dying like most people. So through telling about my process over the last 10 years and this book, hopefully there are some great nuggets to help you reverse the dying process like it did me and to find freedom and stay free.

THE FREEDOM
BEFORE THE PRUNING

Hebrews 4:12

" For the word of GOD is alive and active, sharper than any double-edged sword. It penetrates even to dividing soul and spirit, joints and marrow; it judges the thoughts and attitudes of the heart.

Mark 2:22

"And no MAN putteth new wine into old bottles: The new wine doth burst the bottles, and the wine is spilled, and the bottles will be marred: But new wine must be put into new wine bottles."

So I started out by asking why I would start on this process. I named this chapter 'The Freedom before the Pruning' because years ago I wanted the freedom before the process. Let me tell you a little about my life and how it all got started. Well, it started out good, I guess, because God gave me life. At the age of 2 years old, my life started to be sharpened. My earthly father left our lives. My Mother and he split up and went their own ways. My Dad was a drinker and did not love my Mom, so she was looking in all the wrong places and faces. We all have a void in our lives that belongs to our Maker. It is so vital for the children. I know now. Why did I need to start the process? To get the dead stuff out and bring on life so I could live and not die. I was running in this world and was of this world for the first 45 years of my life, and one Sunday afternoon I started this path to freedom. I saw the passion of Christ where JESUS died on the cross for me. Keep in mind I was like most people; (I had) no REAL peace, no REAL joy, nor good fruit in my life. I had enough of the pain of this life in the world's way. There is no gray area in this thing called life. Half in and half out was not working for me, meaning serving my GOD part time. All that comes from the world's way is pain. Trust me, I know. I will tell you most of the process. Was it worth it? Yes, it was. Was it easy most of the time? No. Will I be in the process for the rest of my life until I pass through or JESUS comes back to get me? Yes, I will and like Paul in the Bible tells me, I have to die to myself DAILY. Over the last 8 to 10 years I have discovered a lot of things through the process. The pruning had to take place before I got the fruit and freedom in my life! And through the word of GOD is where my process started.

In Hebrews 4:12 it says "For the word of GOD is alive and active, sharper than any double-edged sword; it penetrates even to dividing soul and spirit, joints and marrow; it judges the thoughts and attitudes of the heart." So what the Word of GOD did for me was to start the process to the PEACE in the inner man. I found out the Word of GOD did the surgery on my inner man that needed to be done BADLY! I also found that I needed to be working harder on the inner man more than anything else. I always worked on my outer man, trying to get it right and when I started working on the inner man the outer man started to be transformed. What I found out: the more pruning I did through the word of GOD - the more good fruit came into my life. And that is what I have found out also, we prune trees and bushes for the same reason we prune our lives, to get new growth. The old growth that was in my life was stopping the new growth. Like it says in Mark 2:22, "you cannot put old wine in new wineskins" meaning I had to get rid of the old thing that was not working in my life before I could bring in the new. Trust me, I found out that this process will not start or happen on its own. I was like the man sitting in front of the stove waiting for heat but was not doing anything to get the heat. I discovered that, like that man, I have to go get wood and put it in the stove and then light the wood to get heat.

There were 3 main reasons I needed to prune the inner man in me. First, I needed to get rid of the dead stuff that was killing me. Like a tree, you have to get rid of the dead limbs to get new growth and to keep the living part of the tree growing. If you have more dead than living in a tree the tree will die over time because the tree is still trying to feed the dead part of the tree. If you do not get the dead out of the tree, it will die! The 2nd reason was to make room for spiritual growth. We are like trees, if we don't remove the dead limbs on a tree or bush it can kill the rest of the tree or bush. (In the same way, if we don't remove parts of our lives that don't bear fruit we may end up feeling dead inside, or worse - actually dying.) Pruning brings new growth and fruit to our lives as it would for a tree or a bush. I am in the pecan business and every year after harvest time they prune the top of the trees so that the tree can produce new fruit. (Once we have removed the dead in our life, we have more time, money, and mental space to allow for new growth.) The third reason I needed to prune my inner man was that I had so much dead growth in me I couldn't hear what the Holy Spirit was saying most of the time! I needed to prune any dead limbs in me to hear what GOD was saying to me through the HOLY SPIRIT so I could get the good fruit to grow in my life!! It says in 1 Corinthians 6:19 "Or do you not know that your body is a temple of the Holy Spirit within you, whom you have from GOD? You are not your own." I had to prune and clean up this body that was on loan from GOD. My body is more than just the physical body, it is also made up of GOD's mind, GOD's will, and GOD's spirit .And after I pruned I had to really watch what I was letting into my spirit. It says in the word that when a house is clean (they are talking about the inner person) the spirit that left will bring back 7 times more evil than was cleaned out if we do not get something good to occupy that space. That is why the Bible is a great place to start after the cleaning. I'll explain this more as we go back eight years ago and talk about the process I went through.

WHY GOD?

Jeremiah 29:11 "For I know the plans I have for you, declares the LORD, plans to prosper you and not to harm you, Plans to give you hope and a future."

Proverb 10:22 "The blessing of the LORD brings [TRUE] riches, And GOD adds no sorrow to it [For it comes as a BLESSING from GOD]"

2 Chronicles 16:9 "For the eyes of the Lord run to and fro throughout the whole earth, To show HIMSELF strong on behalf of those Whose heart is loyal to him?."

John 10:10 "The thief cometh not, but for to steal, and to kill, And to destroy: I AM come that they might have life, and that they might have it more ABUNDANLY!!!!!"

Why not GOD? People think that GOD is mad and mean. I heard a man say one time, "We think GOD is the one out to get us, JESUS is the one protecting us, and the Holy Spirit is the weird one you need to stay away from.

I have heard people that know nothing about GOD ask why a loving GOD would send people to hell. Now that I have walked more with GOD, I wonder why a person would pick hell over a loving GOD. GOD is my source; everything I have is because of Him. From the air I breathe which is a BIG one to the feet that carry me, it all comes from GOD. I changed my mind about GOD after I stopped thinking of Him like my earthly father. I used to think my Heavenly Father acted like my earthly fathers. I used to play the blame game; I would blame others because it was easier to live with myself. I had to prune that from my life and start to hold myself accountable for my life. That is where I got the understanding of free will. It is my free will that was making and breaking me.

I look at it like this now. I always thought GOD put stuff on me to teach me something. I found out something through this journey I have been on. I found out that, no, GOD does not do that, He really doesn't have time for that when I look around and I see all the goodness of GOD from the nature that He created for us to enjoy. I know it was my free will that was making me and breaking me. Nature means the phenomena of the physical world collectively, including plants, animals, the landscape, and other features and products of the earth, as opposed to humans or human creations. This has GOD all over it...the physical force regarded as causing and regulating these phenomena. I think at times in my life, GOD wishes He did not give me free will because of the way I used it and then blamed Him for the bad that came out of it... meaning the decisions I was making with my free will. I am not going to give this a lot of time but I think it needs to be talked about. Where does the bad come from, then? John 10:10 says the devil comes to kill and steal and to destroy: JESUS said I have come that they might have life, and that they might have it more abundantly. And if He is giving life why would He give life and then put sickness or anything else on me to teach me something? "I am the good shepherd: the good shepherd giveth His life for the sheep." So this is why I know GOD gave me free will. Just like everything else I took my free will and made bad decisions. And GOD gave me all the good things that keep me living the good life for free: the air I breathe, the blood that runs through my veins, the feet I walk on, and the hand that I can pick things up with just to mention a few. It is like the promises of GOD. Now that I know what I know, I ask the question, "Why don't more people look to GOD for all that He is and has done for us?" I found that I was putting value in the things I can buy with money but I can replace all that stuff whenever I want. The things GOD has given me for free I never put any value on. But the day I started putting value on all the gifts that GOD has given me things started changing before my eyes that GOD gave me for free, Yes, for free.! In 2 Corinthians 4:18 it says "so we don't look at troubles we can see now; rather, we fix our gaze on things that cannot be seen. For the things that are seen now will soon be gone, but the things we cannot see will last forever." I pray and then turn it into praise because I found out that GOD inhabits the praise of his people: he lives within our praise. James 1:17 says "every good and perfect gift is from above, coming down from the father of the heavenly lights, who does not change like shifting shadows." I know now that I serve a loving GOD. John 3:16 tell me how much GOD loves me. "For GOD so loved the world that He gave his one and only son, that whoever believes in Him shall not perish but have eternal life." I always stopped there but when I read on, it tells me in John 3:17 "for GOD did not send his Son in the world to condemn the world but to save the world through JESUS." So yes, most of my life, I sat like most people under condemnation most. Then I got the truth through the word of GOD!!! I stayed in bondage for years because of this. I met this guy that said he could not go in to the church because of the condemnation. See, I believed the lies for year and I know now where the lies come from.

Romans 8:1 tells me "There is therefore now no condemnation to them which are in Christ JESUS, who walk not after the flesh, but after the spirit. For the law of the spirit of life in Christ JESUS hath made me, *Anthony*, free from the law of sin and death." So, no, GOD is not mad at us. He loves us unconditionally. Steve from Gateway made a great point one Sunday night about who was sitting on our ground and how to get him off. He said the devil is sitting on most of our property and the only way to get him off is to ask father GOD to help us. And our heavenly father wants us to call on him so he can do that. And yes, Mama, yes, Sir, GOD is not mad at you. The only way we are saved is by grace through faith. GOD loved us first by sending his Son to die for us when we were still sinners. What I had to do was get to know GOD on a personal level. I thank GOD, 8 years ago when I started this process I did not have to unlearn a lot of junk. I did not know GOD. How did I get to know GOD? It is like getting to know any one - you have to spend time with them.

Pruning Versus Discipline--------Which is it?

You can distinguish pruning from discipline by asking a few simple questions. I encourage you to carefully review the accompanying chart. If you suspect that you are being pruned, follow these steps:

1 Acknowledge that GOD is trying to get your attention. Decide that you don't want this season of turmoil to go to waste.

2 Trust that since a loving parent would tell a child why he or she is receiving correction, your loving Father will do no less. Believe that He wants you to know whether you are experiencing discipline or pruning.

3 Ask the Lord to help you answer this question: Do I have a major sin that's causing you to discipline me?

4 Pray, "Lord, I want to know. If You do not show me within a week from today that it is discipline, then I will take it by faith that it is pruning." From my own experience, I can assure you that GOD has many ways to let you know if sin is the issue --- you will find the truth in a Scripture, a conversation, a teaching, or a phone call from a friend.

5 If you conclude that you're being disciplined, sin is the problem. Repent and turn around and change your mind. You'll never regret it.

6 If you conclude that you're being pruned, your response is just crucial, and the rewards will be even greater. Ask God to show you clearly what He wants you to let go of out of your life, and then trust Him enough to release it completely to Him.

Issue	Disciplining	Pruning
How do you know it's happening?	Pain	Pain
Why is it happening?	You are doing something wrong.	You are doing some-thing right.
What is the level of fruitfulness?	No fruit	Fruit
What is your Vinedresser's desire?	Fruit	More fruit
What needs to go?	Sin	Self
How should you feel?	Guilty, sad	Relief, trust
What is the right response?	Repentance (Stop your sinning.)	Release (Give GOD your permissions.)
When does it stop?	When we stop sinning.	When GOD is finished.

IS THERE SOMETHING YOU SHOULD SAY TO GOD?

Imagine a sunny day in Indiana. Darren, twenty–five, has driven up from Memphis to see his dad, whom he's hardly spoken to for years. They're out in the driveway shooting a few hoops. Finally, Darren gets out what he has driven so far to say:

"Dad, I didn't understand you for years. I didn't know why you had so many rules for me in high school-----about parties, TV, chores, driving, money. I didn't like your expectations. I thought you were mean and stupid. I said terrible things about you behind your back. And Dad, I'll admit that I hated you at times. But now I see that you were just trying to be a good dad. You only wanted what was best for me. You never gave up or gave in."

"I came here to apologize for what I have thought and said about you. I was wrong. I know I hurt you very deeply, I'm sorry."

One day I had a conversation with my heavenly father like this and I think we all need to. I remember the day when I finally made amends with God over how I was acting and being towards Him. That was a few years ago, and I can tell you that it has radically improved my relationship with God. Isn't it amazing that God allows Himself to be hurt by us? (We know this happens because Ephesians 4:30 says, "Do not grieve the Holy Spirit.") It's hard to comprehend God's tender love in the face of our misunderstanding, repeated rejection, and unwarranted abuse toward God. Yet, His love remains constant!

If your relationship with God is injured, we serve a Good Good Father. He is ready to forgive us. Just ask. I encourage you to apologize today like I did for my attitude and thoughts towards him. Tell God you have misunderstood His actions and badly misjudged His character. Tell Him exactly how you have felt and why, and ask Him for His forgiveness.

I now pray the prayer of JABEZ. WOW, what a deal!!! GOD wants us blessed!!I ask GOD to bless me every day!!!! HE DOES!!! I PRAY for GOD to give me boldness to do what He has called me to do and help me follow through!!!! I pray that GOD will keep evil and temptation away from me so that I will be free of pain!!!

LET'S TALK ABOUT JESUS FOR A CHANGE

"I am vine, you are the branches.

He who abides in ME, and I in him, bear MUCH FRUIT; for without ME you can do   NOTHING".....................JESUS

Come to Me (JESUS), all you who are weary and burden, and I JESUS will give you REST. Take MY yoke upon you and LEARN of ME for I AM GENTLE and HUMBLE in heart, and you will find REST for YOUR SOUL!!!" ....JESUS

In Romans 10:9-10 it tells me if I will "confess with my mouth the Lord JESUS, and shalt believe in *my* heart that GOD raised JESUS from the dead I will be saved!" The word of GOD says I must go through JESUS to get to GOD. In John 14:6 the word says, "I am the way, the truth and the Life. No one comes to the Father, but through me." Notice that JESUS himself said this. JESUS proclaimed that <u>He</u> is the only way to GOD. So, 8 years ago is when I started the process through **JESUS** to **peace** and **freedom**. It was one Sunday afternoon. I watched the passion of Christ and I THANK the LORD that he did not quit or walk away from the cross, like He could have. Everything I was trying to overcome in my life was taken care of through JESUS on the cross. Like JESUS said, "It is finished." I was looking for a friend and I found one in JESUS. A lot of people are lonely and they have no hope or peace in their lives, but they don't need to live like this because of the finished work on the cross. All we have to do is believe and receive JESUS. JESUS is where I finally found what I was looking for. And this is a big one, Romans 8:37-39 "No; despite all these things overwhelming victory is ours through Christ, who loved us. And I am convinced that nothing can ever separate us from GOD's love. Neither death nor life, neither angels nor demons, neither our fears for today nor our worries about tomorrow. Not even powers of hell can separate us from GOD's love. No power in the sky above or in the earth below, indeed nothing in all creation will ever be able to separate us from the love of GOD that is revealed in Christ JESUS our Lord." John 15:1-4 says "I am the true vine, and my Father is the husbandman. Every branch in me that beareth not fruit he taketh away; and every branch that beareth fruit, he purges it, that it may bring forth more fruit. Now ye are clean through the word which I have spoken unto you. Abide in me, and I in you. As the branch cannot bear fruit of it, unless it abide in the vine." So, JESUS tells me if I stay plugged in to him, GOD will do the pruning and He will bring the fruit into your lives like he did in my life. So please don't miss that point that JESUS made. Getting grafted into JESUS is the way to freedom. JESUS will get you there and keep you there. I found out that is what they do to pecan trees to get better fruit off the trees. They graft them. They take a branch from one tree and graft it to another. Grafting means insert or fix (something) permanently to something else. It was wild to me because one day I was cleaning up pecans under one tree and there were two sizes of pecans. So I asked a man there why one pecan was bigger than the other. He told me that they grafted the tree to get bigger and better pecans. Sounds like what JESUS was talking about in John 15. So what I found out 8 years ago when I got grafted into JESUS' family tree is that then the fruit my life bore was much better in quality and quantity. Yes, John 15 tells us GOD will help us prune the things out of our lives that need to go away to help us to freedom and get the fruit in our lives that we are looking for. What I had to do was be careful when I started the process of pruning the things that I need to prune and get out of my life. I had to make sure I was grafting the right stuff back into my life so I could get the good fruit in my life.

Matthew 12:43 says "When an impure spirit comes out of a person, it goes through arid places seeking rest and does not find it. Then it says, 'I will return to the house I left.' When it arrives, it finds the house unoccupied, swept clean and put in order. Then it goes and takes with- it seven other spirits more wicked than itself, and they go in and live there. And the final condition of that person is worse than the first. That is how it will be with this wicked generation." This is why when I started pruning things out of my life that needed to go away, I needed to graft the right stuff back in and the word of GOD was a great place to do that. Put good stuff in - good stuff comes out!!! Romans 11:17 "But some of the branches were broken off, and you, although a wild olive shoot, were grafted in among the others and now share in the nourishing root of the olive tree." So you want to get nourished and get your life back? Get grafted into JESUS. Get into His promise and stand on the promise of the Word of GOD! Just like trimming trees I know it works! If you will take action it will cause a reaction in your life like it did in mine. There are more people today trying to get the healing fruit in their lives. JESUS is His name and JESUS is the one you are looking for!!! I can do all things through JESUS!!! He is the one that gives me strength!!! Amen!

At the table of grace JESUS mercy is never ending

to me and you! JESUS LOVES US!!!

THE MOST POWERFUL THING
ON THE EARTH TODAY

"Listen carefully: I am sending the PROMISE of my father [the HOLY SPIRIT] upon You; but you are to remain in the city until you are CLOTHED (Fully equipped) with POWER from on high."

The Holy Spirit is our helper.

John 16:13 "When the spirit of truth comes, He will guide you into all the truth, For He will not speak on His own authority, But whatever He hears He will speak, and He will declare to you the things that are to come."

Get some of this before you do anything else. That is what JESUS told the twelve disciples in Luke 24:49. Now remember, this is JESUS talking. So 8 years ago when I stopped taking people's word for what the Word said, I started getting into the Bible for myself. I started focusing and listening to what JESUS was saying to me through His word. And, yes, I think we all need to make it personal because it is.

In Luke 24:49 JESUS said "Listen carefully: I am sending the promise of my Father (the Holy Spirit) upon you; but you are to remain in the city until you are clothed with power on high." What I found out is: that is where peace is. It gave me great peace that passes all understanding that I was looking for when I got filled with the Holy Spirit. And the Holy Spirit pruned the bad out of my spirit. I know now that this was the missing element in my life. It was my way to freedom. How I know... there was lots of pain and no real fruit coming from my life until I got filled with the Holy Spirit. I thought it was funny when people would ask Pastor Robert Morris, "Are you the judge?" and he would say, "No, I am the fruit inspector."

In Matthew 7:20, here is JESUS talking again, "By their fruit you will know them." Now that I know what I know I ask myself why more people don't activate the Spirit in themselves. I just thank GOD now for his free gift and all the other free gifts GOD has given me. Most of these gifts have been used and abused by people. That was what always kept me from the Holy Spirit. But I can tell you this is one of the greatest gifts GOD has given us. What I had to do is work this one out for myself. And now thank GOD I did. What I ask now is why was I singing songs trying to get the Holy Spirit to come down to earth? Matthew 18:20 says "For where two or three are gathered in my name, there am I with them." Galatians 5:22-23 says "but the fruit of the spirit is Love, Joy, Peace, Longsuffering, Gentleness, Goodness, Faith, Meekness, and Temperance; against such there is no law." A friend of mine and I started asking people if they could get one thing in their lives what would it be. The number one answer was peace. And that was one of the things that convicted me to start writing and telling my story. I had found it and knew how to get it. So the missing element I know now was that the Holy Spirit needed to be activated in me. In John 14:26 here is JESUS talking again. I love this guy! "But the Helper, the Holy Spirit, whom the father will send in my name, He will teach all things. And He will help you remember everything that I have told you. My peace I give to you; not as the world gives do I give to you. Do not let your heart be troubled, nor let it be afraid. [Let my perfect peace calm you in every circumstance and give you courage and strength for every challenge.]" I thought the peace came when I saw what they did to JESUS on the cross and I received what JESUS did on the cross. That was only the beginning to my freedom. In Matthew 12:31-33 "There is nothing done or said that can't be forgiven. But if you deliberately persist in your slanders against GOD's spirit, you are repudiating the very one who forgives. If you reject the son of Man out of some misunderstanding, the Holy Spirit can forgive you, but when you reject the Holy Spirit you're sawing off the branch on which you're sitting, severing by your own perversity all connection with the one who forgives. If you grow a healthy tree, you'll pick healthy fruit. If you grow a diseased tree, you'll pick worm eaten fruit." The fruit tells you about the tree. So how do we get a good tree producing good fruit? Well I am glad you asked! Like JESUS told the twelve, get you some of the Holy Spirit!!! Then start the process of pruning all the bad and dead out of your life. The Holy Spirit is our helper. John 16:13 "When the spirit of truth comes, He will guide you into all the truth, for He will not speak on his own authority, but whatever He hears He will speak, and "He will declare to you the things that are to come." I heard my pastor put it this way; the Father wills it, the Son words it, the Spirit works it. If you will agree with the Father's will for your life, and the Son's word for your life the Holy Spirit will work it in your life. Study on the Holy Spirit and then get you some like JESUS told the disciples. You will be glad you did. And, no, the Holy Spirit did not leave with the disciples. Hebrews 13:8 says "JESUS is the same yesterday, today and forever!!!!" Amen

THE BIGGEST SECRET THE DEVIL DOESN'T WANT YOU TO KNOW

1 Corinthians 14:2 "For him that speaketh not unto men, But unto GOD; for no man understandeth [him]; Howbeit in the spirit He speaketh mysteries."

Mark 16:16-18 "He that believeth and is baptized shall be saved; but he that believeth not shall be damned. And these signs shall follow them that believe; In my name shall they cast out demons; they shall speak with new tongues; They shall take up serpents; and if they drink any deadly thing, it shall not hurt them; they shall lay hands on the sick, and they shall recover."

This is the direct line to GOD! Like 1 Corinthians 14:1-4 tells us "Pursue love, and earnestly desire the spiritual gifts. Especially that you may prophesy for one who speaks in tongues speaks not to men but to GOD; for no one understands him, but he utters mysteries in the spirit. On the other hand the one who prophesies speaks to people for their up building and encouragement and consolation. The one who speaks in a tongue builds up himself. The one who prophesies builds up the church." What I love about the word of GOD is that it gives me a way to get through whatever I am trying to get through in this life. The thing about it until I started studying the word and doing what it says to do nothing came from it. It is one thing to just read it and another thing to apply it to my life. In my life it came down to trusting GOD's word and doing what it was telling me to do. And I found out it does work if I work it. And let me say I am not working to get GOD to love me. I am saved by GRACE through FAITH. And I will say no one can work this out for me. I always wanted someone else to do all the studying and then tell me how it goes. That was a bad deal most of the time. It is just like trimming trees. I do not know it all and I will never know it all. When I stay green I grow; if I get ripe I will rot. The fruit from the trees are the same way. I can say that for eight years of applying and working it, I do know that this gift of tongues does work. And what it did in my life - it pruned the bad stuff out of my spirit. Also, it keeps the wrong things off my phone line, my direct line to GOD that is. It clears up that line; it prunes the bad off it. Like I said after 45 years my line was stopped up, it has cleared up now! I look at it this way now: if it is broken let me get it fixed through the word of GOD! The best thing about it, I have learned if it worked once it will work again. Just like pruning and trimming trees, if it worked one time it will work again. Now if it is not broken I need to stop trying to fix it. I am a lot like Eve in the Bible: I always thought there was something better until I got there. And there has been a fire. "Those who believe in my name (JESUS) they will cast out demons; they will speak in new tongues; they will pick up serpents with their hands; and if they drink any deadly poison it will not hurt them; they will lay hands on the sick and they will recover." Let me say you do not have to speak in new tongues to be saved. When I started digging in the word of GOD and studying and started finding all that GOD had promised me in his word and I started applying it to my life, it set me free and it continues to keep me free. I think we think when we get saved and that that is all. And we do not receive the rest of the gifts GOD wants us to have. It is like buying a car with no motor in it, you can sit in it but there is no gas pedal. And the Holy Spirit and tongues are the gas and the gas pedal to get the car moving. I thank GOD that I did not need to unlearn a lot of things when I came to JESUS. This was why it was so important that I got into the word of GOD for myself. Colossians 2:8 "See to it that no one takes you captive by philosophy and empty deceit, according to human tradition, according to the elemental spirit of the world, and not according to Christ." This is why I needed to get into the word of GOD for myself. I run into a lot of people that are living in the brokenness and looking for a way to fix the brokenness. I have found out there is only one way to fix the brokenness. It is the word of GOD through JESUS. And yes the brokenness will go away if you start the process.

TEN REASONS WHY EVERY BELIEVER SHOULD

SPEAK IN TONGUES

Mark 16:17 "And these signs shall follow them that believe…they shall speak with new tongues"

Reason 1 --- Tongues, the Initial Sign

ACTS 2:4 "And they were all filled with the Holy Ghost, and began to speak with other tongues, as the spirit gave them utterance."

Reason 2 --- Tongues for Spiritual Edification

1 CORINTHIANS 14:4 "He that speaketh in an unknown tongue edifieth himself."

Reason 3 --- Tongues Reminds us of the Spirit's Indwelling Presence

John 14: 16-17 "And I will ask the Father, and he will give you another Helper (Comforter, Advocate, Intercessor - Counselor, Strengthener, Standby), to be with you forever - the spirit of Truth, whom the world cannot receive because it does not see Him or know Him, but you know Him because He (the

Holy Spirit) remains with you continually and will be in you."...JESUS

Reason 4 --- Praying in Tongues is Praying in line with God's Perfect Will

ROMANS 8:26-27 "Likewise the Spirit also helpeth our infirmities: for we know not what we should pray for as we ought: but the spirit itself maketh intercession for us with groanings which cannot be uttered."

Reason 5 --- Praying in Tongues Stimulates Faith

JUDE 1:20 "But ye, beloved, building up yourselves on your most holy faith, praying in the Holy Ghost."

Reason 6 --- Speaking in Tongues, a Means of Keeping Free From Worldly Contamination

1 CORINTHIANS 14:28 "But if there be no interpreter, let him keep silence in the church; and let him speak to himself, and GOD."

Reason 7 --- Praying in Tongues Enables Us to Pray For the Unknown

Reason 8 --- Praying in Tongues Gives Spiritual Refreshing

ISAIAH 28:11-12 "For with stammering lips and another tongue will he speak to people. To whom he said, This is the rest where-with ye may cause the weary to rest; and this is the refreshing: yet they would not hear."

Reason 9 --- Tongues for Giving Thanks

I CORINTHIANS 14: 15-17 "What is it then? I will pray with the Spirit, and I will pray with the understanding. I will sing with the spirit, and I will sing with the understanding also. Else when thou shalt bless with the Spirit, how shall he that occupieth the room of the unlearned say 'Amen' at thy giving of thanks, seeing he understandeth not what thou sayest? For thou verily givest thanks well, but the other is not edified."

Reason 10 --- Speaking in Tongues Brings the Tongue under Subjection

JAMES 3:8 "But the tongue can no man tame; it is an unruly evil, full of deadly poison."

THE GREATEST INSTRUCTION
MANUAL EVER WRITTEN

Matthew 6:33-34 "But first and most importantly seek (aim at, strive after) His kingdom and His righteousness [His way of doing and being right--the attitude and character of GOD], and all these things will be given to you also." So do not worry about tomorrow; for tomorrow will worry about itself. Each day has enough trouble of its own."

We have instruction manuals for everything in our lives. We have an instruction manual for our TV, remote, the DVD player, and the cable box to make the channels come in. We have a manual for our cars and our boats and our refrigerators. There are thousands of manuals to tell us how to work anything. I thought one day that it would be great to have an instruction manual for my life. And it rose up in my spirit that there is an instruction manual for my life and how to get through this life. And the greatest instructor wrote the manual. The Bible is the greatest instruction manual ever written and JESUS was the great instructor that wrote it. My problem was I always read it like any other book until one day I took the instruction of Matthew 6:33 and that is when my life, inner and outer, started to change. And the word of GOD started coming alive to me. And for me that was a great place to start my journey.

Matthew 6:33 gave me great instruction. It says "seek ye first the kingdom of GOD and His righteousness and all things will be added unto you." I know now the Word works if I stay in it and do what JESUS is telling me to do. It's like when I got a hold of Psalm 1:1-3. This was the scripture I first started applying to my life. It gave me great peace and continues to give me instruction on how to keep my life on track and stay free. I know the Word works because I have seen the fruit come from it. And that is the thing about it, if it will work one time it will work again. I look at it this way, if all else fails see instruction in Matthew 6:33. What I love about the Word of

GOD is it is like any instruction manual. If I take the instruction and do what it is telling me to do it will come out the way it says it will come out just like any instruction manual. I will use just one example. In Psalm 1:1-3 GOD is working through David. "Blessed is the man that does not walk in the counsel of the ungodly, nor stand in the way of the sinner, nor sit in the seat of the scornful. But his delight is in the law of the Lord; and in his law he meditates on GOD's Word day and night. And he will be like a tree planted by the river of water, that brings forth his fruit in season; and whatever he does will prosper!!!" They say that 8 to 16% of people are using this instruction manual called the Bible. The thing about it, I had to decide how I was going to apply this to my life and why I was going to apply it to my life. So I am thankful I started the process. It is just like trying to get heat out of a stove. If I don't put wood in and start a fire I am not going to get heat. What I found out was there were years and layers of things in my life that needed to be pruned or cut out. In Israel they said with the grapevine they have to wash the grapevine and keep them clean. If they don't, they have to take a knife and cut the buildup off. That is what the word did for me and keeps doing for me. I wash my inner man with the word and it keeps my spirit clean!

THE PROMISES THAT COME FROM THE INSTRUCTION

2 Peter 1:4 "And because of GOD'S GLORY and EXCELLENCE, GOD has GIVEN us great and precious PROMISES. These are the PROMISES that enable you to share GOD'S divine nature and escape the world's corruption caused by human desires."

Matthew 11:28-29 "Come to me all you who are weary and burdened, and I will give you Rest. Take my yoke upon you and learn from me, for I am gentle and humble in heart, and you will find REST for your soul."

Receive His divine nature and escape the world's corruption caused by human desires.

What is a promise? It's a declaration or assurance that one will do a particular thing or that a particular thing will happen. So let's take a look at one. Matthew 6:33 is the promise of everything being added to me. But I had to take the instruction and apply the instruction to get to the promise. As a young man I always got it backwards. I wanted things to happen before I did anything. I have been in the tree-trimming business for 8 years. This year is the first year I really have thought about this trimming and pruning process thanks to people like Dr. Henry Cloud that GOD is working through. He is the one that got me thinking about this and it is so true about the way it works. I went to a lady's house while it was still winter. All of the branches looked dead. Some of them were. Most of them just needed to be pruned and trimmed back. So as I cut everything back I was thinking, there is no way this is going to come back like it should. But man, you should scc it! All the green and color is taking over. And the lady is happy and all excited. So would it have worked if I did not prune and cut back everything? I found out that these bushes and trees are just like my life. It all depends how and how much I am willing to prune in my life to get my life on track. The instruction here is if I am willing to cut back and prune the old things out of my life - the things that were killing me - the new is coming. If I had not started pruning them out of my life, I would have been dead. The fear of loss is greater than the desire to own. Just like that lady I was working for, she did not want me to cut the green on the bushes and vines in her yard. But that is how you get new growth. I had to cut out some of the living things in my life to get the new to start growing in my life. This means there were people/things that were old and that should have been pruned out of my life years ago that I was hanging on to. Did some of the pruning hurt? Yes, because when you cut something or yourself it hurts. I have found the best tool to prune with is the greatest manual ever written: The Bible. They say there are 8000 promises in the Bible. 8000! Wow! If there are 8000 promises this is the question I started asking myself: "Why all the hurting, sick, down people?" Well, that is why I am writing this book...to let people know what I have found out and that I know now it will work if I will work it. All I have to do is repeat. "You say 'what do you mean?'" Ok, all I have to do if I pruned one day and got some good and successful results is repeat the next day and do the same thing I did the day before! If I get into the Word of GOD and it starts changing me - and it did -all I have to do is repeat how and what I did. Let me say that we live in a microwave society. We want it now! But it is like pruning. It is going to take a while for the new growth to start. As people, we don't start the process or we don't stay in the process. And there are a lot of people so close but they talk themselves out of the process. I know - been there, done that! Here are a few of the promises that GOD has made us.

Matthew 6:33 "Seek ye first (#1) before you do anything else." Yes, first - not second ... first! And then and only then "all good things will be added unto you."

Psalms 1:1-3 If I put good things in the promise is good things will come out of it.

Jeremiah 29:11 "For I know the plans I have for you, says the LORD. They are plans for good and not for disaster; to give you a future and a hope."

Matthew 11:28-29 "Come to me all you who are weary and burdened, and I will give you rest. Take my yoke upon you and learn from me, for I am gentle and humble in heart, and you will find rest for your soul."

And it goes on and on and on......

8

THE 3 M'S THAT WILL HELP YOU PRUNE AND KEEP YOU GROWING!

omans 12:2 "Be not conformed to this world but be ye transformed by the renewing of your mind, that ye may prove what is that good, and acceptable and perfect will of GOD!"

Psalms 1:1-3 is where it really started for me. "Blessed is the man that does not walk in the counsel of the unGODly, nor stand in the way of the sinner, nor sit in the seat of the scornful. But his delight is in the law of the Lord; and in his law he meditates on GOD's word day and night. And he will be like a tree planted by the rivers of waters, that brings forth his fruit in season; and what he does will prosper."

Proverbs 18:21 tells me "life and death are in the power of the tongue, and the ones who love it will eat the fruit of it."

I speak life and not death, blessing not cursing into my life.

GOD knew that the BATTLE was going to be in the MIND. The hill where they crucified JESUS was called Golgotha, that is to say, a place of a skull. And when you look at it, it looks like a skull. So GOD knew our battle was going to be in the mind. The mind is the spirit of the devil's work shop. I found out that is the only place that he can work when I am saved. When I receive what JESUS did on the cross I am covered by GOD insurance!!!! YOU can't touch this!!! M C Hammer has a song and now I think that is what he was talking about!!! If I don't control my mind something or someone else will. So what I found out was that when I control my mind I can and will control how things come out around me. It tells me in Romans 12:2 "Be not conformed to this world but be ye transformed by the renewing of your mind, that ye may prove what is that good, and acceptable and perfect will of GOD!" In James 1:8 it tells me "A double minded man is unstable in all his ways." Living in this fallen world, it is tough at times trying to stay balanced. But the way I have found to do that is through the mind with the Word of GOD. In Psalms 1:1-3 is where it really started for me. "Blessed is the man that does not walk in the counsel of the unGODly, nor stand in the way of the sinner, nor sit in the seat of the scornful. But his delight is in the law of the Lord; and in His law he meditates on GOD's Word day and night. And he will be like a tree planted by the rivers of waters, that brings forth his fruit in season; and what he does will prosper."

I think most people would say, how in the world can I meditate on GOD's word day and night? Well the thing about it is, we are all meditating on something. The mind never sits idle. At least mine does not sit idle.

I always depended on someone else to give me their opinion on what the Word said. When I stopped doing that and started getting into it for myself, things started changing. For me it was one thing to get in and read the Word but the big one that changed my life and gave me the peace I have now, is taking action and applying it to my life. Philippians 4:9 is a great promise from GOD. It says "What you have learned and received and heard and seen in me – practice these things, and the GOD of peace will be with you." What I have learned from the Word is that when I started meditating on the Word of GOD it performed surgery on the inner man in me and activated my spirit and gave me peace. Like Hebrews 4:12 says "The Word of GOD is alive and active, sharper than any double edged sword; it penetrates even to dividing soul and spirit, joints and marrow; it judges the thoughts and attitudes of the heart." So the Word started the pruning process in me. This was a big one for me. Also, Joshua 1:8: This book of the law shall not depart from your mouth, but you shall meditate on it day and night, so that you may be careful to do according to all that is written in it; for then you will have success." Really? Really? And I say now, yes, really. This promise from GOD really works. I had a saying that I had back in 2014; 'No change, no change' and I am starting to bring it back. Because if I want change in my life, I have to do something different. Because if there is no change everything remains the same. They call that insanity - doing the same thing over and over again expecting different results. I was always trying to control what was going on around me. But most of the time I have no control on what is going on around me.

In Proverbs 4:23 it says "Above all else, guard your heart, for everything you do flows out of it." How do I protect my heart? I protect my heart with my mind and mouth. The mind is the gateway to my soul, heart, and spirit. And I am the gate keeper. The mind is one of the most powerful things in us. And what we need to be mindful of is the ANTS, or Automatic Negative Thoughts. I had to control what I was letting in my mind. GOD gave me free will over my life. What I do with the free will has determined how things come out in my life. Whatever I am feeding my mind is going into my soul. What I found out when I started feeding my mind the Word of GOD is that the Word of GOD activated my spirit. Wow! That is where the peace came from in me...the peace that passes all understanding like GOD's Word promised me. My spirit was lying dormant until 8 years ago when I started my journey.

Psalms 1:1-3 is the main scripture that set me free and is keeping me free. As a man told me, I have no control over people or things around me. All I can do is control what I am doing and how I am acting. I am sowing and reaping. Whatever I am sowing is coming back to me the way I am sowing. I believe if I am sowing good stuff, good stuff is coming back to me meaning money, freedom, joy, peace, love. Whatever I am sowing, it is coming back to me the way I am sowing. And seed reproduces of its own kind meaning if I sow apple seeds I am going to get apples.

Galatians 6:6 "Let him that is taught in the Word communicate unto him that teaches in all good things. Be not deceived; GOD is not mocked: for whatsoever a man soweth; that shall he also reap. For he that soweth to his flesh shall of the flesh reap corruption; but he that soweth to the spirit shall of the spirit reap life everlasting. And let us not be weary in well doing: for in due season we shall reap, if we faint not." So I know now, that is why I reap a lot of peace in my life because through my mind I have been sowing the Word into my spirit. I found out whatever I was focused on was bringing things to pass in my life. So what did I have to do? I had to CHANGE MY FOCUS!!!! In Philippians 4:8 it says, "Finally, brethren, whatsoever things are true, whatsoever things are honest, whatsoever things are just, whatsoever things are pure, whatsoever things are lovely, whatsoever things are of good report; if there be any virtue, and if there be any praise, think on these things." So this was a big one for me and it works. So I found out that it has to be a focused thing. The focus will take me where I want to go in my life. The focus will do 1 or 2 things. It brings good or bad. There is no gray area to this I found out. So every day when I get up I have to decide where my focus is going to be for the day. First thing I do is what Matthew 6:33 tells me and that is a great place for me to start. I ask GOD to help me with this and he does. But all day every day I have to be mindful and do my part when it comes to the focus. I found out as a man the three things that will destroy him faster than anything if we have the wrong focus are the lust of the eyes, the lust of the flesh, and the pride of life. And BELIEVE me all three have in the past caused pain in my life. So how do I deal with the lust of the EYES? Simple... don't look! I got that from Pastor Robert. It is called blinders. I need to put them on and keep them on!

So what I had to do was change my focus and be mindful of what I was letting into my mind. And when I changed my focus things started changing around me! Like Jim Rohn said and he was right on, I need to be working hard on the inner man more than the outer. When I started working on the inner man, the outer...meaning the things around me...started changing. And is it going to be an ongoing process? Yes. How did I deal with the lust of the flesh? Self-denial/keeping self in line/not giving into the flesh! I have to die daily to my flesh like Paul tells me in the Word. How could I kill the pride? I did not know until one Sunday when Pastor Jimmy Evans was preaching on pride. I love to praise and worship my GOD and, like he said, when I am praising I am focused on my GOD and not self. So what I discovered is that the fastest way to kill pride is through PRAISE and Worship. This 'M'...the mouth...is the one that always got me in trouble. But now I am on a 60-second rule with myself that has really helped me. I learned this from Allen Pickering, my counselor, and it really works for me when I am mindful of it. I found out after 60 seconds I am not effective if I keep talking. But on the other hand pertaining to my life, Proverbs 18:21 tells me "Life and death are in the power of the tongue, and the ones who love it will eat the fruit of it. I speak life and not death, blessing not cursing into my life." So when I came across this scripture I said let's see if this works. I was really tired of eating sour grapes. I started changing the words that were coming out of my mouth. And yes, I can say it does work when I watch or be mindful of my words. Like it says in Mark 11:23 (this is JESUS talking) "Truly I tell you, if anyone says to this mountain, go throw yourself into the sea and does not DOUBT in their heart but BELIEVES that what they say will HAPPEN it will be done for them." I found out that I needed to be speaking to all the mountains in my life about how big and great my GOD is…Not speaking to my GOD about how big my mountains are. See, we have not given GOD a chance. GOD wants us to ask because we have not because we ask not. I had to ask my GOD to help me remove those mountains in my life. Somehow, I was like most people thinking GOD was mad at me trying to teach me something. He was a mean BAD GOD that was mad at me, I thought. So I had to decide which is bigger: my GOD or my mountains. I started looking around and seeing how BIG my GOD is. Matthew 12:37 (JESUS is talking to me here) "By my words I shall be justified and by my words I shall be condemned." So that tells me GOD has given me free will over my words like he did with my life. I found out: change my words change my life. James 3:10 tells me "Out of the same mouth proceed blessing and cursing." So I had a decision, did I want to be blessed or cursed? My choice! And when I got the right things coming out of my mouth it started working in my faith. "Faith comes from hearing and hearing comes through the Word of GOD!" So I had to start speaking or hearing the Word of GOD and STOP listening to the entire negative thing coming from people and the world. "Faith is the substance of things hoped for, the evidence of things not seen yet." I found out if I am speaking life, life is coming and if I am speaking death, death is coming like JESUS was telling me. It is one way or the other - no gray area here. Like Psalm 45 tells us: "My tongue is the pen of a ready writer." So the way I started looking at it and found out, I cannot be speaking negatively and get the positive and good fruit to come into my life. It is like oil and water - they don't mix.

HOW TO GET THE FREEDOM AND KEEP IT.

Romans 10:9-10 says "If I confess with my mouth the LORD JESUS and I believe with my heart that GOD has raised JESUS far from the dead, I will be saved!"

2 Corinthian 3:17 "Now the LORD is the SPIRIT, and where the SPIRIT of the LORD is there is FREEDOM"

Romans 8:2 "For the law of the spirit of life has set you free in CHRIST JESUS from the law of sin and death"

John 8:36 "So if the SON sets you FREE, YOU will be FREE indeed"

Number 1: The way to freedom is JESUS! Romans 10:9-10 says "If I confess with my mouth the Lord

JESUS and I believe with my heart that GOD has raised JESUS from the dead, I will be saved!"

For the first 45 years of my life I lived in the world and was of the world. I saw so much pain in the world and I experienced so much in my own life. I asked myself, was I really saved? And I say now, yes, but not FREE like GOD wanted me to be. It was because there was no true FRUIT coming from my life. JESUS has always been the best thing going. See, what I had to stop doing was comparing my earthly fathers to my heavenly father. It is like that dying tree. It is dying because of all of the dead in it. If the dead isn't pruned or removed, one dead limb starts the process to death. And it is the same way with my life. I had to get the dead out. I found out - the more I got into the instruction manual (the Bible) and did what it says to do, the more things changed in my life. I had to start applying it to my life to get the CHANGE. NO CHANGE...NO CHANGE. It is just like everything in life. I had to start to work everything out for myself through JESUS. When I got ready, my teacher was always there! They say when the student is ready, the teacher will appear! And that is good news. I know now it is one thing to read it and another to apply it to my life. No action...no reaction.

Matthew 7:13-14 (this is JESUS talking and this is the way my life was) "Enter through the narrow gate. For wide is the gate and broad is the road that leads to destruction, and many enter through it." JESUS is talking about the worldly way here. There is a lot of destruction in the world's way. "Small is the gate and narrow the road that leads to life and only a few find it." I look at this scripture and it explains the pain in this life that is all around us. There is a book and it is called the Bible. I call it the great instruction manual. There are only 8 to 16% of people that get it out and read it. That means there are probably an even smaller percentage of people who are putting it to use and doing what it tells them to do. So how did I get to the freedom in the inner man? The Bible! And this is how I have been and still am pruning and getting the dead out of my life. The Father wills it, the Son words it, and the Spirit works it.

I must agree with the Father's will for my life, the Son's Word for my life and the Holy Spirit's works in my life. So what do I think is the way to keeping freedom in my life?

I know that I know that I know…no doubt in my mind about this! Receive JESUS and what he did on and through the cross! Renew your mind every day with the Word of GOD and get filled with the Holy Spirit! Don't take my word for it. It is not my word anyway, it is GOD's Word!

FIND A WAY EVERY

DAY TO SPEND

QUIET TIME WITH

GOD.

HE AWAITS YOU!

www.ingramcontent.com/pod-product-compliance
Lightning Source LLC
Chambersburg PA
CBHW051332120626
46547CB00016B/2509